The
★ The ★
UNITED
STATES
PRESIDENTS

Donald TRUMP

Jake Lee

Big Buddy Books
An Imprint of Abdo Publishing
abdopublishing.com

abdopublishing.com

Published by Abdo Publishing, a division of ABDO, PO Box 398166, Minneapolis, Minnesota 55439.
Copyright © 2017 by Abdo Consulting Group, Inc. International copyrights reserved in all countries. No
part of this book may be reproduced in any form without written permission from the publisher. Big Buddy
Books™ is a trademark and logo of Abdo Publishing.

Printed in the United States of America, North Mankato, Minnesota
112016
012017

Second Edition March 2017

THIS BOOK CONTAINS
RECYCLED MATERIALS

Design: Sarah DeYoung, Mighty Media, Inc.
Production: Mighty Media, Inc.
Editor: Paige Polinsky
Cover Photograph: Dreamstime.com
Interior Photographs: Alamy (pp. 13, 17, 19, 21, 27, 29); AP Images (pp. 5, 7, 9, 25); Seth Poppel/Yearbook
    Library (pp. 6 left, 11); Shutterstock Images (pp. 6 right, 15, 23)

Publisher's Cataloging-in-Publication Data

Names: Lee, Jake, author.
Title: Donald Trump / by Jake Lee.
Description: Minneapolis, MN : Abdo Publishing, 2017. | Series: United States
    presidents | Includes bibliographical references and index.
Identifiers: LCCN 2016954384 | ISBN 9781680783629 (lib. bdg.) |
    ISBN 9781680790511 (ebook)
Subjects: LCSH: Trump, Donald, 1946- --Juvenile literature. | Presidential
    candidates--United States-- Biography--Juvenile literature. | Political
    campaigns--United States--Biography--Juvenile literature. | Presidents--
    United States--Biography--Election, 2016--Juvenile literature.
Classification: DDC 973.932/092 [B]--dc23
LC record available at http://lccn.loc.gov/2016954384

Contents

Donald Trump 4

Timeline 6

Early Life 8

Off to School 10

Work and Family 12

Building an Empire 14

Tough Times 16

Politics and TV 18

Political Success 22

Winning! 26

President Trump 28

Office of the President 30

Presidents and Their Terms 34

Glossary 38

Websites 39

Index 40

Donald Trump

On November 8, 2016, Donald Trump was elected the forty-fifth US president. Trump was a famous businessman and TV star. However, he had little **political** practice.

Trump planned to bring jobs to the United States. He said he would reshape **immigration**. And he promised to put America first.

Trump's supporters were excited by these ideas. Others were concerned about his lack of experience. Americans waited to see how he would lead.

Timeline

1946

On June 14, Donald Trump was born in New York City.

1968

Trump **graduated** from college.

1983

Trump Tower opened.

1987

Trump's first book, *The Art of the Deal*, was released.

2015

In June, Trump announced he would run for US president.

1999

Trump first ran for US president.

2004

Trump began hosting the TV show *The **Apprentice***.

2016

On November 8, Trump was elected the forty-fifth US president.

Early Life

Donald John Trump was born on June 14, 1946, in New York City, New York. His parents were Fred and Mary. Donald had two brothers and two sisters.

Fred worked in **real estate**. He was very successful. Even so, he taught his children to work hard and not waste money.

★ FAST FACTS ★

Born: June 14, 1946

Wives: Ivana Zelníčková (1949–), Marla Maples (1963–), Melania Knauss (1970–)

Children: five

Political Party: Republican

Age at Inauguration: 70

Years Served: 2017–

Vice President: Mike Pence

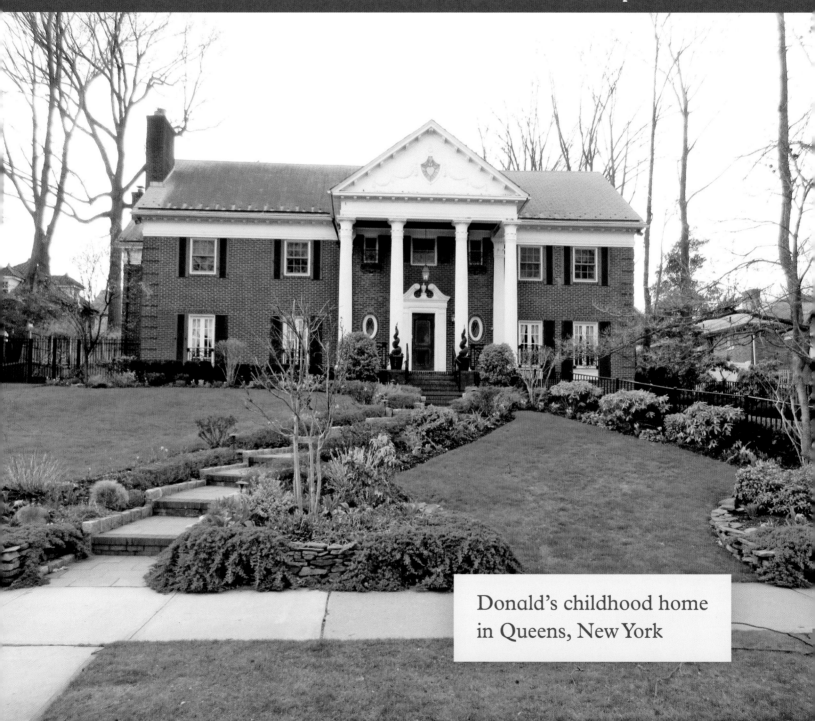

Donald's childhood home
in Queens, New York

Off to School

Donald attended Kew-Forest School in Forest Hills, New York. There, he was known for being loud and bold! He often got into trouble. So when Donald was thirteen, his parents sent him to a military school.

Military school was hard for Donald. There were many rules. Still, Donald did well. He became a sports star. He played soccer, baseball, and football. He was known for his leadership ability.

Donald attended New York Military Academy for five years. He was made a captain for a short time as a senior.

11

Work and Family

Trump finished military school in 1964. Next, he went to college in New York and then Pennsylvania. Trump **graduated** in 1968. He went to work for his father at Trump **Organization**.

At work, Trump oversaw his father's rental properties. He also began increasing the company's holdings. By 1973, he was president of the Trump **Management Corporation**.

During this time, Trump's family also grew. In 1977, he married Ivana Zelníčková. The two had three children, Donald Jr, Ivanka, and Eric.

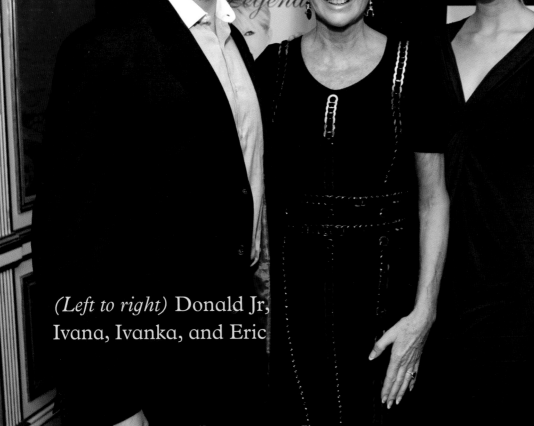

(Left to right) Donald Jr, Ivana, Ivanka, and Eric

Building an Empire

Through the 1970s and 1980s, Trump continued buying properties. His company also built new buildings. Trump became known for his ability to make deals.

In 1983, Trump opened Trump Tower. At the time, this was the tallest all-glass building in New York City. It held offices, homes, and stores. The Trump family lived on the top three floors.

In 1987, Trump wrote about his life. The book was called *The Art of the Deal*. Trump had become a well-known public figure.

Trump Tower is 58 stories tall.

Tough Times

In the late 1980s, the US **economy** was struggling. Trump lost a lot of money on his properties. He had to borrow money to pay bills.

Trump also faced personal struggles. In 1992, he and Ivana **divorced**. The next year, Trump married Marla Maples. The two had a daughter they named Tiffany. They divorced in 1999.

By the mid-1990s, the economy had improved. In 1996, Trump bought the Miss **Universe Organization** with TV **network** NBC. It produced several **beauty pageants**.

Marla Maples *(right)* and Tiffany Trump. Maples was the host of two Miss Universe pageants while married to Trump.

17

Politics and TV

In 1999, Trump began turning from business to **politics**. That year, he began his first presidential run. He hoped to be chosen by the **Reform Party** in the 2000 election. However, Trump did not have enough support. So, he dropped out of the race.

Meanwhile, Trump soon found fame on TV. In 2004, Trump began hosting The **Apprentice**. On the show, individuals fought for a job with Trump's company. The show made Trump even more famous.

Trump received a star on the Hollywood Walk of Fame for his work on *The Apprentice*.

In 2005, Trump founded Trump **University**. It allowed students to take online **real estate** courses. That same year, he married Melania Knauss. The couple had a son they named Barron.

In 2008, Trump's show was renamed *The Celebrity Apprentice*. On it, celebrities fought for money for **charity**. The show continued to draw viewers. But Trump was preparing to move his attention to an even wider audience.

★ DID YOU KNOW? ★

Trump loves to play golf! He owns 17 golf courses.

The last show of Season 14 of *The Celebrity Apprentice* was held at Trump Tower. Barron attended with his dad.

Political Success

In 2011, Trump wanted to run for president as a **Republican**. But he did not get enough support. Four years later, he announced he would run in 2016.

During the race, Trump gave a speech on ending illegal **immigration**. Some people were uncomfortable with Trump's ideas. So, several **organizations** stopped working with him.

But Trump's supporters liked his message. He stood for a change in **politics**. He promised to "Make America Great Again."

Trump has been a member of three political parties. They are Reform, Democratic, and Republican.

TRUMP

TEXT "TRUMP" to 88022

St. Louis, Missouri

MAKE AMERICA GREAT AGAIN!

However, Trump suggested building a wall along the country's border with Mexico. He also wanted to ban **Muslims** from entering the US. Some voters were concerned this might lead to **discrimination**.

Despite this disagreement, Trump was the **Republican** party's choice to run in the election. He would face **Democrat** Hillary Clinton.

The 2016 election was very ugly. Both sides made unfavorable claims about one another. Clinton was widely favored to win. But Trump did not quit. He traveled the country speaking to voters right up to Election Day.

Clinton had been First Lady, Secretary of State, and a Senator from New York.

Winning!

On November 8, 2016, Americans cast their votes. Clinton was ahead in most polls before Election Day. But when the votes were counted, Trump had won!

In his victory speech, Trump said he would improve the nation's **infrastructure** and **economy**. He assured the people he would put America first. He understood some voters were unhappy. He asked them to come together. He promised to be president of all Americans.

Trump's wife Melania held the Bible as he was sworn in as president.

President Trump

On January 20, 2017, President Trump took office. Right away he signed laws to improve the **economy**, control **immigration**, and fight **terrorism**.

On February 28, President Trump spoke to Congress. He discussed his accomplishments. He explained his future plans. He promised to put America first and keep its citizens safe.

Democratic members of Congress did not support him. But President Trump continued his message of unity. He asked all citizens to embrace a renewal of the American spirit.

On his first day as president, Trump filed the paperwork to run for reelection in 2020.

Office of the President

Branches of Government

The US government has three branches. They are the executive, legislative, and judicial branches. Each branch has some power over the others. This is called a system of checks and balances.

★ **Executive Branch**

The executive branch enforces laws. It is made up of the president, the vice president, and the president's cabinet. The president represents the United States around the world. He or she also signs bills into law and leads the military.

★ **Legislative Branch**

The legislative branch makes laws, maintains the military, and regulates trade. It also has the power to declare war. This branch includes the Senate and the House of Representatives. Together, these two houses form Congress.

★ **Judicial Branch**

The judicial branch interprets laws. It is made up of district courts, courts of appeals, and the Supreme Court. District courts try cases. Sometimes people disagree with a trial's outcome. Then he or she may appeal. If a court of appeals supports the ruling, a person may appeal to the Supreme Court.

Qualifications for Office

To be president, a candidate must be at least 35 years old. The person must be a natural-born US citizen. He or she must also have lived in the United States for at least 14 years.

Electoral College

The US presidential election is an indirect election. Voters from each state choose electors. These electors represent their state in the Electoral College. Each elector has one electoral vote. Electors cast their vote for the candidate with the highest number of votes from people in their state. A candidate must receive the majority of Electoral College votes to win.

Term of Office

Each president may be elected to two four-year terms. The presidential election is held on the Tuesday after the first Monday in November. The president is sworn in on January 20 of the following year. At that time, he or she takes the oath of office.
It states:

> I do solemnly swear (or affirm) that I will faithfully execute the office of President of the United States, and will to the best of my ability, preserve, protect and defend the Constitution of the United States.

Line of Succession

The Presidential Succession Act of 1947 states who becomes president if the president cannot serve. The vice president is first in the line. Next are the Speaker of the House and the President Pro Tempore of the Senate. It may happen that none of these individuals is able to serve. Then the office falls to the president's cabinet members. They would take office in the order in which each department was created:

Secretary of State

Secretary of the Treasury

Secretary of Defense

Attorney General

Secretary of the Interior

Secretary of Agriculture

Secretary of Commerce

Secretary of Labor

Secretary of Health and Human Services

Secretary of Housing and Urban Development

Secretary of Transportation

Secretary of Energy

Secretary of Education

Secretary of Veterans Affairs

Secretary of Homeland Security

Benefits

★ While in office, the president receives a salary. It is $400,000 per year. He or she lives in the White House. The president also has 24-hour Secret Service protection.

★ The president may travel on a Boeing 747 jet. This special jet is called Air Force One. It can hold 70 passengers. It has kitchens, a dining room, sleeping areas, and more. Air Force One can fly halfway around the world before needing to refuel. It can even refuel in flight!

★ When the president travels by car, he or she uses Cadillac One. It is a Cadillac Deville that has been modified. The car has heavy armor and communications systems. The president may even take Cadillac One along when visiting other countries.

★ The president also travels on a helicopter. It is called Marine One. It may also be taken along when the president visits other countries.

★ Sometimes the president needs to get away with family and friends. Camp David is the official presidential retreat. It is located in Maryland. The US Navy maintains the retreat. The US Marine Corps keeps it secure. The camp offers swimming, tennis, golf, and hiking.

★ When the president leaves office, he or she receives lifetime Secret Service protection. He or she also receives a yearly pension of $203,700. The former president also receives money for office space, supplies, and staff.

PRESIDENTS AND THEIR TERMS

PRESIDENT	PARTY	TOOK OFFICE	LEFT OFFICE	TERMS SERVED	VICE PRESIDENT
George Washington	None	April 30, 1789	March 4, 1797	Two	John Adams
John Adams	Federalist	March 4, 1797	March 4, 1801	One	Thomas Jefferson
Thomas Jefferson	Democratic-Republican	March 4, 1801	March 4, 1809	Two	Aaron Burr, George Clinton
James Madison	Democratic-Republican	March 4, 1809	March 4, 1817	Two	George Clinton, Elbridge Gerry
James Monroe	Democratic-Republican	March 4, 1817	March 4, 1825	Two	Daniel D. Tompkins
John Quincy Adams	Democratic-Republican	March 4, 1825	March 4, 1829	One	John C. Calhoun
Andrew Jackson	Democrat	March 4, 1829	March 4, 1837	Two	John C. Calhoun, Martin Van Buren
Martin Van Buren	Democrat	March 4, 1837	March 4, 1841	One	Richard M. Johnson
William H. Harrison	Whig	March 4, 1841	April 4, 1841	Died During First Term	John Tyler
John Tyler	Whig	April 6, 1841	March 4, 1845	Completed Harrison's Term	Office Vacant
James K. Polk	Democrat	March 4, 1845	March 4, 1849	One	George M. Dallas
Zachary Taylor	Whig	March 5, 1849	July 9, 1850	Died During First Term	Millard Fillmore

PRESIDENT	PARTY	TOOK OFFICE	LEFT OFFICE	TERMS SERVED	VICE PRESIDENT
Millard Fillmore	Whig	July 10, 1850	March 4, 1853	Completed Taylor's Term	Office Vacant
Franklin Pierce	Democrat	March 4, 1853	March 4, 1857	One	William R.D. King
James Buchanan	Democrat	March 4, 1857	March 4, 1861	One	John C. Breckinridge
Abraham Lincoln	Republican	March 4, 1861	April 15, 1865	Served One Term, Died During Second Term	Hannibal Hamlin, Andrew Johnson
Andrew Johnson	Democrat	April 15, 1865	March 4, 1869	Completed Lincoln's Second Term	Office Vacant
Ulysses S. Grant	Republican	March 4, 1869	March 4, 1877	Two	Schuyler Colfax, Henry Wilson
Rutherford B. Hayes	Republican	March 3, 1877	March 4, 1881	One	William A. Wheeler
James A. Garfield	Republican	March 4, 1881	September 19, 1881	Died During First Term	Chester Arthur
Chester Arthur	Republican	September 20, 1881	March 4, 1885	Completed Garfield's Term	Office Vacant
Grover Cleveland	Democrat	March 4, 1885	March 4, 1889	One	Thomas A. Hendricks
Benjamin Harrison	Republican	March 4, 1889	March 4, 1893	One	Levi P. Morton
Grover Cleveland	Democrat	March 4, 1893	March 4, 1897	One	Adlai E. Stevenson
William McKinley	Republican	March 4, 1897	September 14, 1901	Served One Term, Died During Second Term	Garret A. Hobart, Theodore Roosevelt

PRESIDENT	PARTY	TOOK OFFICE	LEFT OFFICE	TERMS SERVED	VICE PRESIDENT
Theodore Roosevelt	Republican	September 14, 1901	March 4, 1909	Completed McKinley's Second Term, Served One Term	Office Vacant, Charles Fairbanks
William Taft	Republican	March 4, 1909	March 4, 1913	One	James S. Sherman
Woodrow Wilson	Democrat	March 4, 1913	March 4, 1921	Two	Thomas R. Marshall
Warren G. Harding	Republican	March 4, 1921	August 2, 1923	Died During First Term	Calvin Coolidge
Calvin Coolidge	Republican	August 3, 1923	March 4, 1929	Completed Harding's Term, Served One Term	Office Vacant, Charles Dawes
Herbert Hoover	Republican	March 4, 1929	March 4, 1933	One	Charles Curtis
Franklin D. Roosevelt	Democrat	March 4, 1933	April 12, 1945	Served Three Terms, Died During Fourth Term	John Nance Garner, Henry A. Wallace, Harry S. Truman
Harry S. Truman	Democrat	April 12, 1945	January 20, 1953	Completed Roosevelt's Fourth Term, Served One Term	Office Vacant, Alben Barkley
Dwight D. Eisenhower	Republican	January 20, 1953	January 20, 1961	Two	Richard Nixon
John F. Kennedy	Democrat	January 20, 1961	November 22, 1963	Died During First Term	Lyndon B. Johnson
Lyndon B. Johnson	Democrat	November 22, 1963	January 20, 1969	Completed Kennedy's Term, Served One Term	Office Vacant, Hubert H. Humphrey
Richard Nixon	Republican	January 20, 1969	August 9, 1974	Completed First Term, Resigned During Second Term	Spiro T. Agnew, Gerald Ford

PRESIDENT	PARTY	TOOK OFFICE	LEFT OFFICE	TERMS SERVED	VICE PRESIDENT
Gerald Ford	Republican	August 9, 1974	January 20, 1977	Completed Nixon's Second Term	Nelson A. Rockefeller
Jimmy Carter	Democrat	January 20, 1977	January 20, 1981	One	Walter Mondale
Ronald Reagan	Republican	January 20, 1981	January 20, 1989	Two	George H.W. Bush
George H.W. Bush	Republican	January 20, 1989	January 20, 1993	One	Dan Quayle
Bill Clinton	Democrat	January 20, 1993	January 20, 2001	Two	Al Gore
George W. Bush	Republican	January 20, 2001	January 20, 2009	Two	Dick Cheney
Barack Obama	Democrat	January 20, 2009	January 20, 2017	Two	Joe Biden
Donald Trump	Republican	January 20, 2017			Mike Pence

"What separates the winners from the losers is how a person reacts to each new twist of fate." Donald Trump

★ WRITE TO THE PRESIDENT ★

You may write to the president at:
The White House
1600 Pennsylvania Avenue NW
Washington, DC 20500

You may e-mail the president at:
comments@whitehouse.gov

37

Glossary

apprentice (uh-PREHN-tiss)—a person who learns a trade or craft from a skilled worker.

beauty pageant—a contest in which people judge a group of women or girls and decide which one is the most beautiful.

celebrity—a famous person.

charity—a group or a fund that helps people in need.

corporation—a large business or organization that follows a specific purpose.

Democrat—a member of the Democratic political party.

discrimination (dihs-krih-muh-NAY-shuhn)—unfair treatment, often based on race, religion, or gender.

divorce—to officially end a marriage.

economy—the way that a country produces, sells, and buys goods and services.

graduate (GRA-juh-wayt)—to complete a level of schooling.

immigration—the act of leaving one's home and settling in a new country.

infrastructure—the basic framework of public society. It includes a community's government, transportation, and education systems.

management—direction of the work of a person or a group.

Muslim—a person who practices Islam.

network—a group of TV or radio stations that broadcast at the same time.

organization—a group that is put together to accomplish a particular goal.

politics—the art or science of government. Something referring to politics is political. A person who is active in politics is a politician.

real estate—the business of selling buildings and land.

Reform Party—a US political party founded in 1995.

Republican—a member of the Republican political party.

terrorism—to use violence to threaten people or governments.

universe—all existing matter and space.

university—a school a student may attend after finishing high school. A university is often made up of several colleges.

★ WEBSITES ★

To learn more about the US Presidents, visit **booklinks.abdopublishing.com**. These links are routinely monitored and updated to provide the most current information available.

Index

Apprentice, The **7, 18, 19**

Art of the Deal, The **7, 14**

beauty pageants **16, 17**

birth **6, 8**

books **7**

Celebrity Apprentice, The **20**

character **10, 26**

children **8, 12, 16, 20**

Clinton, Hillary **24, 26**

Democratic Party **23, 24, 28**

education **6, 10, 11, 12**

election **4, 7, 26**

family **8, 12, 13, 14, 15, 16, 17, 20, 21, 27**

Hollywood Walk of Fame **19**

immigration **4, 22, 24**

Miss Universe Organization **16, 17**

Muslims **24**

New York City **6, 8, 14**

New York (state) **8, 9, 12**

Pennsylvania **12**

political experience **4, 18, 22, 24, 26, 28**

real estate **8, 12, 14, 16, 20**

Reform Party **18, 23**

Republican Party **8, 22, 23, 24**

television **4, 7, 16, 18, 19, 20, 21**

Trump Management Corporation **12, 14**

Trump Organization **12, 18**

Trump Tower **6, 14, 15**

Trump University **20**